# Why You SUCK at Archery

## Praise for
## Why YOU Suck at Archery

"What an enlightening read! A real page turner for any archer serious about improving their prowess. Archers should read this book not once, not twice, but many times! It is written with a tongue in cheek approach, but when you are in the process of reading it, you will swear that the author has seen you shoot and has sat right there during your shooting sessions, too. I'm reading "Why You SUCK . . ." again and literally falling off the couch laughing my butt off! What is really good is that each of the three times I've read it, I've picked up something of an even better perspective. The short and concise chapters make this easy. If you don't purchase this dandy book, you are missing something really good."

*Tom Dorigatti*
50 years in archery, writer for Archery Focus magazine and others, Author of "The Puzzled Archer" and "ProActive Archery"

"Lots of people will tell you that you "suck" at archery (or many other things in your life) but few will give you any good techniques to actually help you do something about it (they secretly don't want you to get better than they are.). Steve Ruis tells you what to do in this book to make your mind better! But you have to read it first and then "take action" to actually apply what you learn so you don't "suck" at archery any longer. Steve, as do all good coaches – actually wants you to get better. So make the move—read this book, improving you thinking and take action!"

*Larry Wise*
International Coach, former world champion, and author of numerous books and DVDs on archery
(Core Archery, How to Tune Your Compound Bow, and others)

I appreciated the ease with which I was able to read this book. The terminology used I could relate to. Not being an archer of caliber at this point in time, easly understanding of what is being said is something I really look for. No problems there. Steve made it seem like he was assessing me right on the line. (How did he know I sucked by the way?) I really found the mental aspect of the archer very useful. I believe that this portion helped me more than any other part of the book. Hit me right at my level of skill and I will recommend it to most of the archers I know!

*Mark Cooper*
Pekin, IL

Steve Ruis

# Why You SUCK at Archery

**by Steve Ruis**

v

Steve Ruis

## Library of Congress
## Cataloging-in Publication Data

Why YOU Suck at Archery / Steve Ruis.
  p. cm
  ISBN 978-0-9848860-3-6 (softcover)
  1. Archery. 2. Training. I Steve Ruis 1946-

ISBN: 978-0-9848860-3-6

The web addresses cited in this text were current as of August 2012,
unless otherwise noted.

**Writer:** Steve Ruis; **Copy Editor:** Steve Ruis; **Proofreader:** Claudia
Stevenson; **Cover Designer:** Claudia Stevenson; **Book Designer:** Steve
Ruis; **Photographers** (cover and interior): Steve Ruis and Claudia
Stevenson unless otherwise noted

Printed in the United States of America 10 9 8 7 6 5 4 3 2 1

**Watching Arrows Fly**
3712 North Broadway, #285
Chicago, IL 60613
312.505.9770
*www.watchingarrowsfly.com*

WATCHING ARROWS FLY, LLC

# Contents

# Introduction

I figure I have about two to three pages of this book to convince you that I know why you suck at archery and convince you that I can help you change that, so I can't afford to beat around the bush. Here are many of the reasons you suck at archery. If any (or many) of these apply to you, you will find a chapter of this book that addresses what you can do to change that. In the second half of the book I explain how to create a killer mental program, the lack thereof is the prime reason you suck at archery.

In no particular order . . .

### You Suck at Archery Because . . .

- **You think archery is 90% mental.**
  The wisest thing I have ever heard about this was from Coach Larry Wise who said that "Archery is about one-third physical, one-third equipment, and one-third mental." Now, if you take care of the physical training and equipment selection and setup ahead of time, what remains (during competition) is about 90+% mental, but if you have equipment or physical flaws of form or execution, no mental game can make up for those.
- **You think archery is 90% mental and then don't practice the mental tools needed.**
  Hey, you aren't alone in this stupidity.
- **You seek advice in all of the wrong places.**
  You seek shooting advice from your buddies, you seek equipment advice from your Pro Shop and from magazines . . . and the Internet, sheesh. It's a good thing you can't put a bow to your head and pull the trigger, like a pistol.
- **You take advice you shouldn't.**
  You are paying a coach for lessons but this guy you met at the range had this great suggestion so you went ahead and changed your bow's

1

setup. He must have had a nice smile! (What the... ?)

- **You'll spend thousands on equipment but not a dime on coaching.**
Tiger Woods has a coach, Kobe Bryant has coaches, Joe Montana hired a *quarterback* coach for his college-bound son, but ... what do they know?
- **You tinker incessantly with your shot.**
In archery, you have to repeat and repeat and repeat your shot. Now, just what is that shot ... this week?
- **You don't practice properly.**
You go to the range, shoot arrows until you string together a longish string of "good shots" and call it a "good practice." You aren't quite hopeless, but close.
- **You don't practice with a plan.**
You don't want to do this, this is what all the top pros do! Move along, there is nothing to see here.
- **You don't write anything down.**
You were a genius in school, so you take no notes, make no lists, and make no plans. You keep it all in your head. It's amazing your head doesn't explode from all the stuff that's in there. Oh, it leaked out you say? No? What, you can't remember!
- **You don't have a shot routine.**
Even golfers have a shot routine! Could that be what's holding you back? D'ja think?
- **You complain about your scores but don't know *how* to score.**
With only a few points separating winners from losers, you can't afford to give away points, yet you give away several if not dozens each round and you have no idea why.
- **You show up at a tournament having forgotten to bring something important.**
Hey, if it were really important, you would have remembered! Now ... where can you borrow some arrows?
- **You stray from your routine under pressure.**
Hey, I've got an idea! I'm going to invent a new way to shoot ... right now. After all only the tournament is at stake!
- **You think a new piece of equipment will make you a better archer.**
If this *were* really true (as much as the equipment manufacturers secretly want you to believe it) and the new bow/release aid/sight/stabilizer you bought will make you X% better than you were, the guy who beats your brains out every tournament will also

have one and since he is already better than you his X% will be bigger than yours and you'll fall even further behind! (And his was probably donated to him by a sponsor.)

+ **You think you are just a couple of good tips away from where you want to be.**
Stockbrokers make very good livings off of people who believe in tips, so do professional archers. If you start thinking tips will help, the next thing you will fall for are "archery secrets!" (There are no secrets in archery.)

+ **You'd rather walk naked down Main St. than let a shot down.**
Sure this shot feels less than perfect but I'm feeling lucky—is that your thinking?

+ **You shuffle your feet between shots.**
Hello? If you found the perfect spots for your feet for the previous shot, your reason for moving them is. . . ?

+ **You go to the range, take your bow out of its case and just start banging away.**
Nothing could have happened to it since the last time you shot it . . . nah, no real reason to check it over.

+ **You believe in magic.**
Carbon is like bacon, it makes everything better. Yeah, right.

+ **You believe your 70# hunting bow should be just fine for target competitions.**
I wonder what the 112th arrow's gonna feel like? Medic!

+ **You think what works for "that guy" just has to work for you.**
Yeah, like I gotta work on my "take off from the free throw line windmill slam" cuz it works so well for LeBron.

+ **You are completely unrealistic about your chances to win.**
You could win this competition, you really could. And while you are thinking about that, I have this bridge you might want to buy.

Have any of these struck the mark? Did any of these hit home? Are you guilty of any of these? Gasp, all of them?! Well, what you going to do, sit and mope? All of these issues can be fixed and it is not too hard to do so. But as Hall of Fame golfer Bobby Jones said: "Competitive golf is played mainly on a five-and-a-half-inch course, the space between your ears." The same is true about archery. You need to just use your head a bit better and you will not only not suck at archery any more, but you will start surprising people.

And won't that be fun?

Oh, that brings up a couple of other reasons why you suck at archery:
- **You are not having fun.**
  If you want to win, losing is not fun. So, why are you approaching everything the same way you did before you got the desire to start winning?
- **You are having too much fun.**
  We have names for archers who only do things for fun . . . recreational archers and, uh, well, losers. When you get to the point that winning is a big part of the fun, you have to rethink how you go about things and doing some things that aren't fun is part of that.

But wait, this isn't all . . . there's more!

# ━━→ Section 1 ←━━

# What to Do to Stop Sucking at Archery

Steve Ruis

# → 1 ←

# You Suck at Archery because . . . you think archery is 90% mental.

I agree with my friend Larry Wise who said that "Archery is about one-third physical, one-third equipment, and one-third mental." If you take care of the physical training and equipment selection and setup ahead of time, what remains (during competition) is about 90+% mental, but if you have equipment or physical flaws of form or execution, no mental game can make up for those.

*So, how can you be sure your equipment is "good enough"?* I said "good enough," because your equipment doesn't need to be the best, nor does it need to be new, it just needs to be "good enough," meaning that it doesn't limit your performance. Obviously, if you are shooting a bunch of bent, mismatched aluminum arrows, replacing them with straight, properly spined arrows will improve your scores. (See, you can "buy a better performance!") But once your equipment is properly fitted to you and tuned, it should be so good that it doesn't limit your performance. One way to tell is just by tracking your group sizes. If your goal is to shoot perfect "300" scores indoors and your groups at 18 m and 20 yds are larger than the highest scoring ring, then you aren't going to make it. If you have tuned and tuned your bow and arrows and the groups won't get any smaller no matter how much you practice, then maybe you should investigate different equipment.

*How do you know you are physically ready to compete?* Assuming the "equipment's 33%" is good enough, how do you know if your form and execution are good enough? Again, tracking group sizes is the key. If you want to shoot "300" consistently in the NFAA five-spot target, then your five-arrow group size at 20 yards has to be less than the diameter of the spot and you have be able to do that every time.

7

You need to shoot practice rounds under competition conditions to prove to yourself you can do it. See Chapter 21 *"You are completely unrealistic about your chances to win"* for ideas of how to determine what your actual chances of winning are.

If . . . and it is a *big* if . . . you have both the physical and the equipment aspects of shooting handled, than yes, what remains is 90% mental. But if your sight marks aren't perfect, if your arrows aren't undamaged, if . . . , if, then all bets are off.

# ➤ 2 ⬅

# You Suck at Archery because . . . you think archery is 90% mental and then don't practice the mental tools needed.

Jeez, do you really expect these tools to be effective without you practicing them? And how do you know which of those tools *actually work* . . . work for *you*? And what are those tools; do you even know?

This failure to prepare is the greatest reason why archers suck, so I have provided a major section on how to create a killer mental program (which is below and, no, don't just jump ahead, there's stuff you need to learn before you can do that; settle down, have some patience, for Pete's sake). For now . . . most archers don't do a lick of work on their mental games until they have done everything they can think of with their form, execution, and equipment and still are losing. Then, they think "maybe there is something in this mental hoodoo, after all." Hello? Wake up and smell the coffee. How many guys do you think have got their equipment and their shot right? Hundreds? Thousands? So, what separates the winners from the losers? (I assume you have noticed that the same guys keep winning, and winning, and winning? Do the names Jesse Broadwater, Reo Wilde, Jaime Van Natta, and Brady Ellison ring any bells?)

The archer who is physically prepared and *is the most mental tough* stands the greatest chance of winning. Consider Dave Cousins, who has been at or near the top of the compound world for as long as I can remember. Mr. Cousins went to Sweden for the world field championships . . . unfortunately his equipment didn't make it. He borrowed a bow, arrows, and a release from a teammate and guess who was in

9

first place after day one? Yep, Mr. Cousins.

Being mentally tough means being able to execute one's mental program under any circumstances. And how do these archers who win and win and win do that?

They practice it.

To help you learn what and how, see Section 2—*How to Create a Killer Mental Program* below. (No, not now, when you get to it. Sheesh!)

# ➤ 3 ◀

# You Suck at Archery because . . . you seek advice in all of the wrong places.

Archery is a social sport and all of us give advice from time to time, even the some of us who shouldn't. If you take advice from all and sundry who have advice to offer, you are doomed, done, put a fork in you. You need to find just a few sources of archery advice you can trust. Everything else you pick up (and I do recommend you always be on the lookout for things you think will help you), you must . . . absolutely must . . . run it past your trusted few to get their opinions.

Face it, if you knew enough to be able to evaluate everything coming your way, you wouldn't suck at archery.

I have to tell you a story. I was at the Vegas Shoot one time, sitting just opposite the Carter Enterprises booth and I watched a guy argue with Jerry Carter for over twenty minutes. The gist of the argument was this yahoo wanted to buy one of Carter's new releases and Jerry wouldn't sell it to him. Jerry said (over and over): "You don't need a new release; you need to learn how to shoot the one you've got." Here's the guy who created the company that makes the best release aids in the world, who makes his living selling the danged things, telling this guy that he wasn't going to sell him something he didn't need.

You'd think the guy would listen, don't you?

He didn't and that is one of quite a few reasons that guy sucks at archery. (I went over to Jerry afterward and told him I would have sold the idiot three releases, just to teach him a lesson. But then, unlike Jerry Carter, I am not a nice man.)

11

If you can get information from an unimpeachable source, I'd listen and listen hard. And I'd still would want to talk it over with "my guys."

I don't want to disparage pro shops, because most of the time you can get pretty good advice about equipment at one. But I can't tell you how many times I have sent students to shops and had them come back with ill suited, wrong headed, stupid stuff. You need to learn who at the shop knows what they are talking about and who is just working their way through school with a part-time job.

And run whatever you are told through "your guys."

➤ *4* ◄

# You Suck at Archery because . . . you take advice you shouldn't.

In mathematics there are tools to determine if any path is completely random or whether there is a pattern to it. The random path is lovingly referred to as "the drunken sailor's walk." You may not realize it, but you are on a path which you hope leads to archery excellence (or at least "archery better"). If you take advice from every Tom, Dick, and Harry who has something to say, you are approximating as closely as is humanly possible, that drunken sailor's walk.

You aren't going anywhere . . . and you're making good time!

If you are smart enough to seek out a coach for lessons, you should run everything you think through that coach. You're paying him; put him to work! If it doesn't work out, then fire him, but don't sabotage what he is trying to do for you by changing things he doesn't approve first.

If you do want to continue to take random advice, then you aren't even on a path; you've reached your destination: you suck and will continue to do so.

Steve Ruis

## ➤ 5 ◄━

# You Suck at Archery because . . . you'll spend thousands on equipment but not a dime on coaching.

This is more of an affliction of the compound side than the recurve side and it has a lot to do with the lack of large numbers of quality archery coaches, but . . . you knew there was a "but" coming din'tya . . . a good coach can save you a lot of grief. If no good coach is available locally, seek one out farther away. (I had a student here in Chicago who went to Arizona to work with a coach and a local youth went all of the way to Korea.) If you build a relationship with a coach who isn't all that near where you live, then later you can work together at a distance. You can talk on the phone, email one another, send video clips via the Internet, that kind of thing.

Good coaches can see things that you can't because they are look-ing from the outside in and are trained to see flaws in your form and execution. I have a hard time at shoots now, because I see too much wrong in most people around me and can't say anything. (First rule of coaching is don't offer advice unless asked.) Drives me nuts!

If you can't find a coach, ask an elite or professional archer to help. And expect to pay them! Whatever idiot came up with the idea that coaching should be free should be taken out and shot. If you get free coaching, you are getting exactly what you paid for! See Chapter 3, above.

# → 6 ←

## You Suck at Archery because . . . you tinker incessantly with your shot.

If you are serious about being good and not sucking at archery, you have to get "your shot" right and then you have to own it. If you don't do this—and most archers do not—you are spending lots and lots of practice time practicing shooting arrows some other way than the way you'll end up shooting arrows. Why practice doing it wrong?

This is where a good coach or serious shooter can save you a lot of time and effort. They can help you figure out how you should be shooting: getting your form right, getting your execution right, getting your equipment right. Then you need to shoot and shoot and shoot until "your shot" is second nature to you.

Most archers shoot and shoot and shoot in the hopes of discovering their shot. Much of that effort is wasted and, in fact, you will hear top coaches say that they spend most of their time working with archers who have taught themselves bad habits. That work is getting back from where you never should have gone, so all of that money and effort was wasted.

Once you get your shot down, then don't change things without full consideration of what will happen. For example, if you change your brace height (tiller, nocking point location, stance, whatever), you just changed everything and need to completely sight in again. You may even need new arrows or need to retune the ones you have. Do not make frivolous changes!

*If you do want to make a change, do it as an experiment.* (Yes, Igor, pass me the Allen wrenches!) Determine what your average score is in some

17

practice round. Then make the change and practice for a while and then shoot some more practice rounds. Did your average go up? No? If not, then it was a *change* all right, it just wasn't an *improvement*. If yes, your average score did go up, then you know that change was worthwhile and you can trust it.

Putting this much effort into evaluating changes means you should not make small change after small change after small change like you have been doing as this can only move you away from "your shot" to something less effective.

Don't spend all your effort getting out of holes you have dug yourself.

Get it right.

Get it down.

Don't tinker frivolously.

# → 7 ←

# You Suck at Archery because . . . you don't practice properly.

You go to the range, shoot arrows until you string together a longish string of "good shots" and call it a "good practice." You aren't quite hopeless, but close.

Don't get me wrong, I thought this is what practice was for years, until I asked a few questions. For example, how many practice rounds should you shoot? *Answer* Not as many as you think, maybe once a week, plus or minus. Most professional compound archers do the bulk of their practice blank bale. (Yes, Bubba, that blank bale, the one without the target.) David Butler (NFAA Outdoor National Champion, AMFS in 1998 and 1999) was famous for having a target bag hanging from a rafter in his shop. He kept a five gallon bucket(!) full of practice arrows and shot them at quite close range. Sometimes he would hike the bag up so he could practice shooting uphill.

Wha? Just stood there shooting arrows into a target bag? Yep. From the outside it looks like just physical exercise. But it is what was going on in his head that was special. He tried to feel every moving part of the bow. He tried to feel what was different about shooting uphill from shooting level. He tried to feel his release. (He once told me that you really get a feel for a bow when you shoot it until it falls apart! Egad!) He was also experimenting with his equipment, testing various setups to see whether *this* worked better than *that*. Maybe once a week he would go to a range and shoot for score. He usually measured practice in how many *buckets* he shot (but with quite a number of goals in mind while doing so).

Professional archers know how to setup their bows within a gnat's eyelash of where they want them in short order. (They have to be able

19

to do this; they get a new damned bow every year from their bow sponsors.) And they still experiment with different releases, stabilizers, sights, apertures, you name it. The rest of the time they spend mostly in shooting blank bale, honing their form and execution. From time to time, they shoot practice rounds.

About the only time they shoot a lot of practice rounds is when they are trying to evaluate a new bow. One professional showed me a notebook of his in which he had recorded the scores (and X-counts and more) of over 35 Vegas indoor rounds testing whether the bow he got from a new sponsor shot as well as his old bow. (It didn't and he went back to his old bow sponsor.) Those rounds were shot with different tunes, techniques, and interspersed with calls to the factory and other pros who were shooting that bow.

# → 8 ←

# You Suck at Archery because . . . you don't practice with a plan.

You don't want to do this, this is what all the top pros do! Move along, there is nothing to see here.

Buy a cheap notebook (see Chapter 9) and start writing (yes, *writing* Bubba, you just can't remember all of the stuff you need to) . . . specifically writing down *practice plans*. Write one for every practice you have. Take just this simple step and you are on the correct path . . . away from sucking at archery.

The kinds of things you want to schedule on your practice plans are: tuning sessions, equipment evaluations, sight mark acquisition and checking, form elements that need work (usually with drills), execution elements that need work (usually with drills), tournament preparation, and practice rounds.

If you want a real shock, write down how many minutes you actually work at each of the things you schedule . . . without including BSing with friends, soda breaks, wandering around the Pro Shop floor/clubhouse, reading archery magazines, fiddling with your smartphone, or any of the other things you do while "practicing." You may be in for a shock at how little time you actually spend practicing.

Here's an archery secret no one else has ever told you. It comes from the world of dieting. It seemed that every attempt to re-educate folks onto healthier diets failed in time. People on healthier diets felt better, lost weight, all the good stuff, but then they would go back up to their old "too heavy" eating habits. Do you know what finally worked for these folks? They were asked to simply *write down* what the ate, how much they ate, and when they ate it. They were shocked at what they learned. And they changed their behavior because they had a tool to show them what they were *really* doing rather than what they *thought* they were doing.

This will work for your archery, too. More on this in Section 2—*How to Create a Killer Mental Program.*

*An Archer's Friend*

## ━━▶ 9 ◀━━

# You Suck at Archery because . . . you don't write anything down.

You were a genius in school, so you take no notes, make no lists, and make no plans. You keep it all in your head.

I know a zillion guys who do this! And they are all missing out. Every measureable part of your bow should be measured and written down where you can find it. (I recommend cheap, spiral-bound note-books.) You don't have to have been in archery very long to have tinkered with a bow until it almost doesn't shoot any more. Gosh, I wish I could put that thing back where it was when it was shooting well! Well, you could if you had measured it up and written it down. Several guys I know use a standard form to contain that information. Any time they change something they fill out a new form (and keep the old one). I hand out copies of these forms to my students when they get a new bow.

When it comes to tournaments, they say that experience is the best teacher. But what the heck good is it if you can't remember what happened? After each tournament write down all of the things you learned . . . about the venue, about the sponsor, about the organizers, about your equipment, about the weather (Gee, Arizona is windy!), about how you shot, . . . everything. Then write down three things or more (but *at least* three things!) that you would do differently the next time you attend that competition.

Those notes help direct your practice in the weeks to come and certainly help you prepare for the next tournament and really help the next time you go back to that venue.

23

Steve Ruis

# ➤ 10 ◄

## You Suck at Archery because . . . you don't have a shot routine.

Even golfers have a shot routine! Could that be what's holding you back? D'ja think?

A *shot routine* or *shot sequence* is just a series of steps you follow to make a shot the first time you approach the shooting line. These are standard operating procedure for all repetition sports. (Note the clever CSI reference, eh?) In archery, a shot sequence allows you to look at the various segments of your shot and work on them individually. The rule of thumb is that each phase of your shot should be at about the same level of quality. Just like a chain is no stronger than its weakest link, your shot is no better than its weakest part. If you strengthen a link already strong enough, you haven't made the chain any stronger. But if you find the weak ones and strengthen them. . . . There are drills available to work on various aspects of your shot, both form and execution. (I am working on a book, "The Big Book of Archery Drills" but it ain't ready yet!)

Once all of the parts of your shot are at roughly the same level of quality, you must then evaluate your skill level. If your performance is not good enough, then you need to bring each and every step up in quality to reach a new level (typically this is done in the order of the shot sequence, beginning to end).

The most common starting place is this sequence:

1) take your stance
2) nock an arrow
3) set your hands (both bow and string/release)

4) raise the bow
5) draw the string
6) find your anchor
7) aim
8) release, and
9) follow through.

(This is wisely called the "9 Steps.") Now, there is a heck of a lot more going on in any one of these steps than just what the words indicate. Take for example: "2) nock an arrow." In my case, I shoot my arrows in sequence so to "nock an arrow" I must find the correct numbered arrow (2a), pull it from my quiver (2b), nock it in the correct place on the string (2c), with the cock vane properly oriented (2d) and such that I can hear the nock snap onto the string (2e), and set that arrow on the arrow rest (2f). In addition, occasionally I shoot with a clicker, so I have to also position the blade of the clicker on top of the arrow (2g). Each step often has substeps, whatever, included in them.

A good start in figuring out what the best "short list" shot sequence is for you is to make a long list, that is list every single darned thing you do when taking that first shot. This list might be 30-40 elements long! (Do you wiggle your fingers settling them into your hand-held release aid? I do; it helps me find the right place for my fingers and ensures they are as relaxed as they can be.) Then reduce the "long list" shot sequence into a "short list" which is namely those steps which cause you difficulties, or the ones you don't execute the exact same way each shot. Some go so far as to paste their "short list" on the inside of their top limb and read it before each shot . . . because until your shot gets almost automated, you will make the mistakes that will cost you the points that will cost you wins, leaving you muttering "I so suck at archery!" Which you shouldn't say, even though it is true—see Chapter 21 below.

*The Mental Side of a Shot Sequence* Archery is all about how shots feel. But most people don't seem to be focused on what we feel. In fact, being "touchy-feely" just doesn't seem right. Our minds get between us and physical reality in that we "interpret" our physical sensations in ways that are counterproductive in archery.

Ultimately, though, the shot sequence steps are interlaced with a strong mental program. (See, I haven't forgotten.) For each physical step of the shot sequence there is a mental check list and this gives the mind—both conscious (earlier) and subconscious (later)—something to do, something that won't distract or intrude on the shot. Each step also provides a touch point, a point in time where certain physical sensations are checked. In the long run, we become more in tune with the feel of good shots to be able to distinguish them from bad ones.

So, here are what archers tend to focus on in their shot sequence.

| Shot Sequence Step | Mental Check |
|---|---|
| 1. Take Your Stance | feet shoulder width apart, toes on line to target, everything relaxed |
| 2. Nock an Arrow | see arrow on rest, cock vane out, hear snap of nock, release hooked onto D-loop |
| 3. Set Your Hands | (bow) on pad of thumb, knuckles at 45°— (draw) fingers set on release so that everything else is relaxed |
| 4. Raise Your Bow | bow shoulder stays down, draw elbow up, hands stay put/relaxed |
| 5. Draw | pull is smooth and crisp with draw elbow up and bow shoulder down |
| 6. Find Your Anchor | peep swings in front of aiming eye, hand touches face near jaw |
| 7. Aim | center scope in peep, check level, focus is on the point you want to hit |
| 8. Release the String | swing draw elbow back and around tripping release |
| 9. Follow Through | hold form (especially line of sight) until the bow finishes it's bow |

(I am using the 9 Steps applied to a compound archer (me) shooting a hand-held release as a model.)

All of these checkpoints are sights and feelings, and they allow me to focus on what I am supposed to see and feel at each stage of the shot. Most of them have to be felt because they are really hard to see when you are zeroed in on the X-ring.

The key mental aspect is: *if anything, anything at all—mental or physical—intrudes from a prior step or from the environment, you must let down and start over.* This I call the Rule of Discipline. You cannot become a winning archer without following this rule. (Cannot, cannot, cannot!) Essentially this rule says that you are *only allowed to shoot shots you know are good shots.* Shooting shots you *hope* are good will not get you into the winner's circle and will guarantee you will continue to suck at archery. The Rule of Discipline is what makes any shot sequence work.

# → 11 ←

# You Suck at Archery because . . . you complain about your scores but don't know *how* to score.

With only a few points separating winners from losers, you can't afford to give away points, yet you give away several if not dozens each round.

So what are the winners doing that you don't? The list is very long, so I can only get you started. The keys are *attitude* and *preparation*. (I know, I know, you've got an attitude . . . but this is different.) For example, when it starts to rain during an outdoor competition, how do you respond? The winners get out their raingear and proceed on. They know that scores will suffer in the rain, but their score is likely to suffer less than others because they are prepared. And, while they don't *like* shooting in the rain, the fact that others will blow themselves out of the competition, because of their bad attitudes, actually makes them happy. (When Peter Elzinga set a new compound world record for the FITA Round (1419/1440) in 2009 it was raining to beat hell for the 90m distance! His first reaction upon looking out the window at the rain was to crawl back into bed.)

Especially in outdoor competitions, you aren't likely to shoot a perfect score, so where do you usually lose your points? How can you minimize those losses? This is what guides the preparation of winners. In the old days, compound archers often shaded their sight marks a little on the high side because they knew that when they got tired near the end of the shoot they tended to shoot a little low. (With modern equipment, arrow speeds are higher and this isn't done so much any more.) Field archers became expert in reading targets. On a downhill 65 yard target most of the arrow holes were on the right side of the tar-

29

get. The shooters on the course were fairly good, so why would that be? Hmmm.

You need to look for every advantage that you can take. Preparing to shoot uphill, downhill, and sidehill shots takes practice. If you don't have such shots on your home range, figure out ways to create them so you can practice them.

If some part of your bow breaks, say your D-loop. Are you done for the day? If something slips out of adjustment, can you find it and, most importantly, can you put that thing back in place *exactly* where it belongs? The minute anything even smells like it may have gotten out of whack, the winners know what to check and how to reset everything with a minimum of lost points. If you don't know what to do, you just keep bleeding points until your are hopelessly behind or you up and quit.

You need to learn these things. You need to measure up your bow so that you know where everything is supposed to be and, best, mark everything so you can tell at a glance if anything is out of place and where to put it back if it slips. Gosh, what can go wrong? I have had release aids jam, servings separate, D-loops break, points come out of arrows, sight knobs stop working, arrow rests come loose, and cable guards come loose. I once even had a cable guard break off during a shot. (That's one I couldn't repair in the field, but I will never, ever use an aluminum cable guard rod again.)

Indoors when you shoot multi-spot target faces, do you shoot them in the same order each time? (If not, you will drop more points than if you do.) Do you deliberately practice next to walls and looking into the face of a left-hander in the next lane so that you will get used to those situations? (If not, you will drop more points than if you do.)

Learning how to shoot well isn't all that hard, learning how to *score* well is a lot tougher. Some of this is based on experience but most of it is based on preparation. Tennis pro Ivan Lendl used to have racquets made up like his opponent used so he could get a feel for how the ball would come off of those rackets when he played those opponents. Now, that's preparation!

If you want to know more about this and shoot a compound bow, check out "ProActive Archery" by Tom Dorigatti.

# ━━▶12◀━━

## You Suck at Archery because . . . you show up at a tournament having forgotten to bring something important.

Hey, if it were really important, you would have remembered! Now . . . where can you borrow some arrows?

Okay, to be fair here, I once showed up at a shoot without my sight. Almost everyone has done something stupid like this. But if you don't want to suck at archery, you can't make a habit of this.

The solution is simple: make a checklist. I have several: one for field events, one for target (outdoor), and one for target (indoor). (I also have checklists for trainings, checklists for seminars, etc.) You don't need a chair or a cooler for field events and you don't need a portable stool for target events, etc. For indoor shoots, your car is a lot closer than for field events, but the things you might need better be in your car . . . and sunscreen lotion isn't one of them!

Hey, making checklists isn't enough . . . you have to use the danged things!

Steve Ruis

# ➤ 13 ←

## You Suck at Archery because . . . you stray from your routine under pressure.

Hey, I've got an idea! I'm going to invent a new way to shoot . . . right now. After all only the tournament is at stake!

As you will learn in Section 2, it is much easier to repeat something you have just done, than to do something for the first time. Being mentally tough means being able to execute your shot, exactly the same way, under very different circumstances. But if your last shot was with an open stance, and now you are going to try the exact same shot with a closed stance, you are nuts!

But you would never do such a thing, would you? Not that, probably, but the little, almost unnoticeable, changes you make in your shot routine under pressure will cost you points and wins. The very first time I was in a shoot-off, I couldn't believe my scope was bouncing up and down so much. Gosh, my first case of tournament jitters! And they were there in every subsequent shoot-off, too. You don't need to be adding self-inflicted handicaps by changing anything in your shot routine to go along with shoot-off jitters when things get on the line.

Fix this by practicing. Imagine you are shooting one or three arrow shootoffs during practice. If you have a shooting partner, compete with them (for a soda or something). If you have a good imagination, you will feel at least of ghost of those jitters. Embrace them! Billie Jean King, in the Tennis Hall of Fame, said that "Pressure is a privilege." It means that you are close to winning. Learn about pressure and how you react to it. And don't screw up by changing anything in your shot you don't have to. Otherwise you will always suck at archery.

33

Steve Ruis

# ➡ 14 ⬅

## You Suck at Archery because . . . you think a new piece of equipment will make you a better archer.

If this were actually true (as much as the equipment manufacturers secretly want you to believe it) and the new bow/release aid/sight/stabilizer you bought will make you X% better than you were, the guy who beats your brains out every tournament will also have one and since he is already better than you, his X% will be bigger than yours and you'll fall even further behind! (And his was probably donated to him by a sponsor.)

Coaches often say "You can't buy better scores." This is not exactly true; you can buy better scores. If your arrows are old and worn, you can buy better scores by replacing them with a matched set (in spine, in weight, in every way). But once you get equipment that is functioning properly and tuned to you, then you really can't buy better scores. You can improve slightly with quality upgrades, mostly with regard to arrows, but those improvements are all small. If you are looking for major shifts upward in score through your credit card, that is a fool's errand.

Practice, grasshopper, practice and preparation. . . .

Steve Ruis

# ➤ 15 ←

## You Suck at Archery because . . . you think you are just a couple of good tips away from where you want to be.

Stockbrokers make very good livings off of people who believe in tips, so do professional archers. If you start thinking tips will help, the next thing you will fall for are "archery secrets!" (There are no secrets in archery.)

There was a time when the top dogs in archery weren't talking. They kept their "secrets" to themselves. Those days are over. There are no secrets any more. If you spend any time with top shooters or a top coach, you will know everything you need to know in short order. Then your job is to execute. This is plain and simple. Occasionally a tip will help you but those occasions are rare. Unless you suck at archery and you haven't read the best sources, or take advice from all the wrong sources, or you just haven't been paying attention, or. . . .

Steve Ruis

# ➤ 16 ◀

## You Suck at Archery because . . . you'd rather walk naked down Main St. than let a shot down.

What are you thinking? Are you thinking letting down is not manly, that it will turn you into a "girly-man?" Listen and listen good, pilgrim: letting down is the manliest thing you can do. You are telling people you can draw twice on a shot and still beat them!

Seriously, you should never, ever shoot a shot you know isn't right. If you do you are just practicing making excuses the next time you should let down. I teach all of my students what I call the Rule of Discipline which says: *if anything, anything at all—mental or physical—intrudes from a prior step or from your environment, you must let down and start over.* No exceptions. Not if you are "just shooting for fun." Not if it is "just practice." Not if you are "just horsing around." Not ever.

If you follow this rule religiously, you will stop shooting most of your bad shots simply because you know those shots are bad before you shoot them.

This is what the pros do. This is what the winners do. If you want to not suck at archery, you have to do this too.

39

Steve Ruis

# ➡ 17 ⬅

## You Suck at Archery because . . . you shuffle your feet between shots.

Hello? If you found the perfect spots for your feet for the previous shot, your reason for moving them was. . . ?

Archery is a repetition sport, more so than bowling, more so than golf. You need to be repeat the exact same shot over and over again (think target archery or indoor archery) from the same distance, in the same conditions, etc. It has been proven scientifically that it is easier to repeat something you have just done than to do something from scratch, so everything about your shot needs to be the same from shot to shot. It is virtually impossible to move your feet and then put them back into the exact same positions, so if you move them, you just changed your stance. Why make things harder? If you are going to shoot X shots from the same position—don't move your feet!

The same thing goes for shooting multi-spot targets, like the Vegas three-spot or the NFAA five-spot target faces. You should shoot the spots on these faces in the same order . . . every time.

Every time you do it is practice for the next time you do it, so why do it differently . . . ever?

Steve Ruis

# ➤18←

## You Suck at Archery because . . . you go to the range, take your bow out of its case and just start banging away.

Nothing could have happened to it since the last time you shot it . . . nah, no real reason to check it over.

A long, long time ago, I took a long airplane flight. Soon after I took my high end camera out to take some pictures and the danged thing was stuck. It cost me a lot of money to discover that vibrations from the airplane caused a small screw to work loose and it rattled around in the camera body, lodging someplace important. Compound bows and even modern recurves have lots of parts held together by screws. They do work loose. When would you like to discover that something is wrong? Half way through a tournament? On target two of a shoot-off? Every time you take your bow out of its case, there should be quick and easy ways to check that nothing has come loose or gotten bent. Check out Tom Dorigatti's book, "ProActive Archery," for ways to do this. (Hey, his book is large and I can't include all of that here!)

Steve Ruis

# ➡ 19 ⬅

## You Suck at Archery because . . . you believe in magic.

Carbon is like bacon, it makes everything better.

Yeah, right.

"New" is not necessarily "improved." Newer and better are not the same thing.

I was talking to a bowhunter the other day and he said that was going to "have to" switch from aluminum arrows to carbon. I asked him "Why?" He said that Easton was discontinuing his old arrows and it seemed to him that everyone was changing, so it must be for a reason.

And I thought "one more lemming headed for the cliff." I asked the guy if he had any problems shooting his aluminums in the field. "Heck no!" was the answer. My response was that there is no reason to drop aluminum shafts if he was happy with them. Just switch to a different model aluminum shaft of the same characteristics and he'd be fine. "Really?" he asked. Really.

Most people change what they are doing because they think there is magic in something else. Golf is even worse at this than archery! "Learn the 'secret move' that will add 30-40 yards to your drives!" "This new driver hits the ball 22% father than our model of just three years ago!" Yada, yada, yada. This is marketing hype! What most golfers never seemed to notice is that the manufacturers of clubs de-lofted the things while adding more length to their shafts. A 3- iron sold now has the same loft that a 2-iron had just fifteen years ago. Experts and machines could indeed hit those clubs longer but it wasn't because of some magic. And those geniuses of golf club design also made the clubs harder for ordinary golfers to use. Most golfers can't hit a 3-iron and certainly can't hit a 2-iron labeled as a 3-iron.

Now, I am not saying archery equipment manufacturers would stoop to such nefarious tactics, but their job is to sell the new stuff they are peddling, not tout how their old stuff was pretty good, too. So they, like everybody else, shout "New, Improved!" I only point out that there is no industry standard definition or standard test for . . . accuracy. Nor is their likely to be (there is no "up side" for the manufacturers, so don't blame them).

So, the next time some shooter tells you that their new, carbon whiz-bang arrows are phenomenal, the best! Ask them what they were shooting before. (Oh, arrows you made out of wood dowels, how interesting.) Ask them how many other brands/models of arrows they tested to come to the judgment that their new thingies are "the best."

There is no magic. Only you can determine if you can work some new piece of equipment better than you work your current rig. Maybe you can borrow one/some to test, hummm?

# ▬►20◄▬

# You Suck at Archery because . . . you believe your 70# hunting bow should be just fine for target competitions.

I wonder what the 112th arrow's gonna feel like? Medic!

The last tournament I was at, guess who won the Freestyle/ Compound Unlimited competition? An old guy pulling 38# peak weight. Heck, a 70# bow is overkill even for hunting but marketing hype has created the situation where that particular draw weight is one of the most common draw weights ordered in new bows. With today's light weight arrows, such loads aren't necessary and they certainly aren't desirable for target use. One expert bowhunter calculated that using a heavy aluminum hunting arrow, a draw weight of a bit over 50# will send an arrow through a Whitetail buck and out the other side, even if you hit a rib.

A 70# bow *can* work for hunting because, well, how many shots do you take on a normal day of hunting? The most typical answers are "none" and "one." Target shooting, on the other hand, requires a lot of shots and drawing way more weight than you need is not an advantage. With a really high draw weight, you are just making yourself unnecessarily tired. Crank it down or better, get another bow just for target. (And, yes, I do know very successful archers who did it with 70# bows, but odds are you aren't one of those guys.)

Obviously, I am talking to compound archers here, but the same thing goes for recurve archers and longbow archers. The biggest obstacle to solid, repeatable form and execution is being overbowed (that is having too high of a draw weight). I see it all the time in my recurve students.

47

Steve Ruis

# ➡ 21 ⬅

## You Suck at Archery because . . . you think what works for "that guy" just has to work for you.

Yeah, like I gotta work on my "take off from the free throw line windmill slam" cuz it works so well for LeBron.

If you are gonna pick somebody to copy, try picking somebody who is your gender, about your height, and level of physical fitness. But, I have a better idea! Archery is not rocket science. There are no "secrets" you can learn by studying "the masters." Why don't you be the best archer you can be. Just skip over trying to be a copy of someone else.

That's it, Bubba, just be yourself.

Steve Ruis

# ➡ 22 ⬅

## You Suck at Archery because . . . you are completely unrealistic about your chances to win.

"Psst, you could win this competition, you really could." I had this thought a great many times . . . and I was just as wrong as you have been. Ordinary thinking goes like this "I could have a really, really good day and all of the other guys could have "off" days and I could win." Thinking like this will leave you believing that rich people have your best interests in mind, politicians will do what is right, and ghosts and fairies are real!

If you want to know how to estimate your real chances, here is how to do it.

*What Are My Real Odds?* The first task is to figure out what it will take to win your tournament. Being blessed with the Internet, we can usually look up last year's winning score for almost any tournament (or better, the winning score for the last three years). If it is not available, ask around the club, pro shop, etc. Once you have that information, you can compare that number with what your average score is. Let's say, just for the heck of it, that the round being shot is a 300 point NFAA indoor round and that the last three winning scores for your competitive category are: 286, 279, and 281. Now, if your average practice score for that round is 264 with your high score being 269 and your low being 254, your average score is about twenty points away from the average winning score of the last three years (283). So, you are not yet in a position to win this tournament. If your average score were 291, you would be in an excellent position to win, but it is not.

To keep it simple, if your average score equals the winning score, you have about a 50:50 chance of shooting a winning score. It doesn't mean you are going to win, but you can, at least, reasonably expect to be "in the hunt."

But maybe you ought to factor in that your competition rounds tend to be 10 points less than your practice rounds. What you don't keep track of both your practice round scores and competition scores?! (Bubba, Bubba, I just don't know what I am gonna do with you.) If you want to have reasonable expectations about whether or not you are good enough to win, you need to keep records (of both competitive and practice scores) and compare them with a reasonable estimate of what it will take to win.

The upside is: if your practice and competitive scores aren't good enough, you need to do the work necessary so that they are, and you now have an idea of what "good enough" to compete is.

Or, what the heck, you could just continue to live in Fantasyland.

# ➤➤ 23 ⬅━

## You Suck at Archery because . . .
## when you lose
## you make excuses.

If you want to take credit when you win, you have to take "credit" when you lose. You could blame your equipment but who, specifically, is in charge of your equipment? There is only one person completely in control of your archery and that is you. If you want to blame somebody, blame the fool in charge!

I know a well-known professional compound archer who makes his own strings and cables because he doesn't want anybody else responsible for his performance. If a cable stretches and it costs him a score, he wants it to be *his* fault. Being responsible means you have to think everything through and take pains to make sure that you are doing everything you can to win. If you make excuses, you are just missing the opportunity to learn how to do things the right way.

The next time you are inclined to blame somebody else or something else for what went wrong, do this little exercise. Write down what you think they did that cost you whatever it cost you. Then figure out what you could have done to prevent that problem. Now which guy/gal do you want to be: the one who has things happen to him, or the one who anticipates such things happening and takes steps to prevent them?

A "no brainer," right?

Realize I am not saying that "stuff doesn't just happen." I've seen guys bleeding copiously because their compound bow's riser broke at full draw and most of the pieces went flying back into their faces. That was not their fault. But anything preventable is your fault, *if you choose*

53

*it to be that way.* This is what the winners do.

# —→24←—

# You Suck at Archery because . . . while shooting, you call yourself names . . . and listen to yourself.

There are plenty of volunteers when it comes to bad mouthing your archery. If you join them, you lose.

Let me ask you a question. Which guy or gal would you like to be like: the person who shows up at a competition brimming with confidence or the one who shows up with doubts about his equipment and form?

Only an idiot would choose to be like the second archer. (Well, maybe that's your problem!) But I have seen more than a few guys get upset about a poor shot and go ballistic on themselves and turn themselves from being the first kind into being the second kind. This is all about what is called "self-talk," basically what you say *to* yourself *about* yourself.

Here's the thing about self-talk. You don't have to buy into psychological mumbo-jumbo about negativity or anything else. It is just this. Your subconscious mind can't tell the difference between bad things you say about yourself to yourself and bad things other people say. Listening to someone else going off as to what an idiot you are doesn't exactly put you into the frame of mind to produce your best work. So, don't do this to yourself.

If something happens that negatively affects your score or placing, whatever, and the source of that is clearly you, going off doesn't help. If it is still early in the competition, you may have enough time to pick up some points and your opponents have time to drop a few, but you do not have the option to continue screwing up, so correct your fault and move on. This is practice for the next time this happens!

Also, don't forget that you are a role model for your adoring fans, or fan, whatever.

# ➡ 25 ⬅

## You Suck at Archery because . . . you think trying harder works.

There is a big difference between *making* a shot happen and *letting* a shot happen. Guess which approach leads to the winner's stand?

Legendary coach John Wooden used to poke fun at people who "gave 110% effort." In his opinion, you couldn't give what you don't have, so 100% effort is the best you can do. The real key, according to Wooden, was figuring out how to get that 100% *consistently*. Aha!

Just what do you think "trying harder" consists of? How do you do it . . . as an archer? I think your best bet is to equate "trying harder" with "screwing up," because in general that's what you'll get. When you make mistakes, you need to train yourself to relax and get back to your shot routine, not "try harder." It helps to have what is called a "recovery program" for this.

*A "Recovery Program" Will Help When Things Go Wrong* Here is an example of what you must do: first, you must stop thinking about the mistake. You must think about something else: a green Chihuahua, an offensive lineman in a tutu, whatever, anything as long as it takes your mind off of the poor shot you just made. Next, you must do something physical, like jostling the arrows in your quiver or tapping your bow or resetting your binoculars, something physical that gets you out of the realm of the entirely mental, then you need to begin the process of engaging the next shot. If you use "cue words" like: "strong bow arm" or "let it float, shoot your shot" such cues can get you mentally into the next shot. According to Troy Bassham of Mental Management Systems (*www.mentalmanagement.com*), this process needs to take at least seven seconds, so don't just rush into your next shot thinking it will wipe away the memory of the bad shot with the

57

image of a good one (that just primes you to repeat the bad shot!). Resetting mentally takes a bit of time. When things go wrong, execute your recovery strategy and get back on track.

I recommend to all my students that they start every shooting session with two things: a couple of let downs (as a reminder that letting down is always an option) and by shooting their shot deliberately and about 10% *slower* than they normally would. This second activity is a first-stage physical recovery program. When you need a recovery program, don't you want to have practiced it just a little while ago? (The shooting warm up moves quickly from the slightly slower, deliberate shots to more flowing shots at normal tempo. Also if you are working on stuff, I insist you go down the list and remind yourself of those things, emphasizing them on your first few shots—otherwise you'll just revert to "normal" form.)

What you are doing right now is thinking about things you do not want to think about—what happens when things go wrong. But if you don't do this ahead of time, you will be stuck doing it, from scratch, every time something does go wrong! So, spend some time developing and practicing your recovery routine. It will give you something positive and constructive to do when things do go wrong. . . .

Instead of doing something stupid, like trying harder . . . whatever that means.

# ➤➤26◀━

## You Suck at Archery because . . . you think a beer belly is just another stabilizer.

If you think what you got hanging over your quiver belt is a competitive advantage, you are going to have to explain how. Go ahead, I'll listen.

I've got one of those waistlines but, hey, I'm over 65 years old and not a threat on the shooting line any more. We used to joke about having such a belly, calling it "archer ballast" which provides front-aft stability to one's stance.

Right.

I am not saying you have to be in great physical shape, that you have to join a gym and lose weight and . . . etc. But take a look at the guys who win all of the time. They tend to be fairly fit. Being physically fit means that you will tire less quickly, that your heart rate will stay low (or at least lower) when under pressure, that you will be able to focus better for longer periods of time.

I'm just saying.

Steve Ruis

# ➤➤ 27 ⬅⬅

## You Suck at Archery because . . . you think about your score while competing.

And exactly how does that thinking help you execute the next shot? Please tell me. (This should be really interesting.)

More good rounds have been killed by thinking about score than you could shake a stick at. (Assuming you . . . had a stick and were in the habit of shaking it at thoughts or ideas!?) If this hasn't happened to you, you are a freak of evolution. Thinking about your score or how you might place, or that you are "winning," or. . . , or anything other than executing good shots, kills performance. Every successful athlete will tell you that and almost all of them learned it from personal experience.

The reason is that those thoughts are major distractions. Nothing in them will help you do what you need to do to make those wishes come true, namely executing good shots.

To be successful, and to not suck at archery, you need to stay in the present moment, not only while you are shooting, but between shots, between ends, during lunch breaks, etc. Which means thinking about anything else, especially fairy tales you tell yourself about your "great score" or "high finish" or "great win" will just ruin those hopes.

Steve Ruis

# ➤ 28 ←

## You Suck at Archery because . . . you *hate* shooting in the wind (heat, rain, etc.).

You don't have to love it (wind, heat, rain, whatever), but it doesn't care what you think and it will effect all archers the same, uh, except those who get bent out of shape, those will be affected the worst.

I am not saying you have to like shooting in the wind, just to not hate it. Same for extreme heat, rain, etc. Part of this is covered by preparation. Having practiced in the wind, or rain, or whatever, you know what to do. You know whether you will "aim off" or use your sight's "bubble" to adjust for the wind. You've set your sights windage and elevation "off" so you have to aim at some place other than the center to practice "aiming off." You've tried on your rain gear and made sure your bowstring doesn't hit the fabric of the sleeve upon release. You are carry thick rubber bands to hold that sleeve material down in case it bunches up. You are prepared.

You have also prepared your attitude. Consider you are having a good time and competing well at an event you typically enjoy. And then the skies darken and it begins to rain. Here are two possible responses to the change in the weather:

*Competitor 1 Says* Oh, no! I hate shooting in the rain! It always lowers my score. There goes my personal best and I probably won't win, either!

*Competitor 2 Says* Oh, I had better get my rain gear out; I'm glad I came prepared. I probably won't shoot a personal best, but I could still win this thing, especially if the two people ahead of me get bent out of shape because of the rain.

We are all capable of the disappointment, disgust, and fear associated with Competitor 1's thought. We are all also capable of learning how to achieve Competitor 2's thoughts with their apparent happiness (came prepared, might win) and reasonable logic (if the two people ahead of me get bent out of shape because of the rain).

This is the question you have to ask yourself: which guy/gal would you rather be?

Is this so hard to do?

I don't think so.

*I did mention a good attitude helps, didn't I?*
*Photo by Claudia Stevenson*

# —→ Section 2 ←—

# How to Create a Killer Mental Program

Steve Ruis

# How to Create a Killer Mental Program

## Introduction

When Chance Beaubouef won Vegas for the second or third time (I can't remember which), he was asked what his best attribute was. He answered "having a strong mental program." Not his bow. Not his release aid. Not his stabilizer. Not his bowstrings. I know I am going on and on, but all of the guy's sponsors claim their particular piece of equipment was the reason he won. But Chance is telling the truth—being able to execute near perfect shots over and over and over requires you to have a strong mind.

So, how do you get a "strong mental program?"

I'm glad you asked because not having one is the prime reason you suck at archery.

## It's About Time, Bubba—No, Really, Time

You are probably thinking it is about time *I* got around to telling you what's needed to make a strong mental program, but likewise the heading of this section could mean it's about time *you* got around to learning the mental side. Really, I need to talk about . . . time. Because time is really, really important.

Let me give you an example. Just think about drawing your bow and then holding your form, at full draw, for say two minutes. Probably at the 20 to 30 second mark you are going to start thinking about shooting me for suggesting this cockamamie exercise. I don't actually want you to do this, but you can see that time is important. Once you raise your bow to start a shot you start using muscle energy at a higher rate (in the muscles used to shoot, of course). If you take too long those muscles will not perform like you want them to and you will take poor shots. Below I will show you how to figure out your best shot timing, but the point here is that the amount of time your shot takes is important.

Equally important is where you place your attention. This is the job of your shot sequence. First you pay attention to taking your stance, then you pay attention to nocking an arrow, then . . . etc. If you find yourself at full draw and you are thinking about your stance, are you gonna get off a good shot? Most people say "no," and they are right. So, your attention must shift *onto* stance, then *off* of stance and *onto* nocking an arrow, then *off* of nocking an arrow and *onto* setting your hands, then . . . etc.

And your attention is limited. Your attention will shift after just a few seconds, so you have to create a list of things to establish the order in which it shifts (the shot sequence) and you can't dawdle, because what happens to, say, your stance when you are at full draw? If you think it is "set it and forget it," you're wrong. I have watched thousands of archers shoot and, if you pay careful attention, you can see all kinds of things going on that are not wanted. I see archers at full draw with their hips opening or closing, with their bow shoulders rising, with their rear elbows dropping. Compound archers, because we spend so much time at full draw are susceptible to all kinds of form flaws creeping in when we aren't paying attention. (You are focused on aiming at full draw, no? Well, you are not paying attention to your hips or feet, then. Me, too. I am not immune.)

So, your attention is limited, your ability to focus is limited, so if we keep the time short, we minimize body parts drifting off doing their own things. Now, we also can't rush through our shots. Think about yanking the bowstring back instead of drawing it back smoothly and strongly. When we yank, we use big muscles and get jerky motions that take time to calm down and we need to expend extra energy getting our sight back on target because there is no way to keep it close while jerking the string around. Rushing is just as bad as moving too slowly.

So, time has to be part of your thinking . . . always . . . and therefore has to be part of your mental program.

## But Wait, There's More . . .

Before I can show you how to create your own mental program, it is important that you understand some basics about how your mind works. (Hey, none of this is perfectly known, especially when it comes to Bubba; this is just the best we understand these things now.)

*Your Conscious Mind Trains Your Subconscious Mind* A key point in understanding an archery mental program is the distinct roles of the subconscious and conscious "minds." (We still don't understand what the heck a mind is; but this is no less useful even so.) There is a saying that "self-consciousness is the enemy of performance." If you remember what it was like to learn to tie your shoes, ride a bicycle, or drive a car, you know what this means. (I still swear the first time I tried to release the clutch on my Mom's car, I got all four wheels off the ground.) When you are fully engaged consciously with a task with which you are unfamiliar, it is a little like herding cats, very awkward and clumsy. But, once you've learned those skills, they become subconsciously controlled and practically effortless. There are some things you need to know about the roles of these two "minds" in learning to shoot arrows consistently.

## The Conscious Mind

The conscious mind is basically your thoughts as you are aware of them. Your conscious mind is very powerful but also very limited. You can really only engage one thing at a time consciously, which gives you the ability to concentrate, a very powerful tool. But it is often the case that our greatest strengths also turn out to be weaknesses. If we were completely mesmerized by what we are focusing on, we probably wouldn't have survived long because predators (Lions, and tigers, and bears, Bubba!) would have snatched us up while we were daydreaming. Because we can't focus for too long on any one thing and survive, it is normal for our conscious focus to flit around. As an example, focus visually on some small thing somewhat near you, try to keep your attention, your focus just on that thing. If you picked something large enough that you could focus on the whole thing, your eyes probably kept moving to take in the whole object, but even if you look at something small, you will find it more and more difficult to focus on just that one thing. It is as if your brain is telling you, "Okay, I got it Bubba; move on; this is dangerous.) You *can* practice focusing—just pick up something small like a release or tab and focus on it. Try to take it all in, the features, textures, etc. When your mind jumps to something else you are done. Start again. Try to stretch the amount of time you are focused on just one thing. There are limits but you can get better, if you practice.

You also may have noticed that all of the other information your eyes were taking in was fuzzy. You only can see clearly in about a 10 degree cone. Outside of that cone, all the way out to the limits of your peripheral vision (often more than 180°) your vision is not sharp at all. If the object of your interest extends beyond this cone of sharpness, your eyes will flit from one part of it to another to another.

Now, that is not the bad news; this is the bad news: *your conscious mind also cannot keep to a single thought for more than about nine seconds.* Try it. Imagine a purple football or a hippopotamus in a tutu, or some other object, and hold it in your mind while somebody times you. When another thought enters your mind, ask for the time and see how long you were able to concentrate. Typically this is less than nine seconds and often much less. At least you now have a reason for why you sucked at math (or whatever subject you sucked at) in school. If presented with a problem and you don't get an idea of what to do next, your mind will wander. Studying and all other mental disciplines are about mastering the art of having your mind wander on task and not onto some more pleasant topic.

## The Subconscious Mind

Keeping it simple, let's just call the subconscious mind all of your mental abilities which operate when you are unaware of doing them. Consider tying your shoes. What do you think about when tying your shoes? Basically anything you want because you don't need to think consciously about tying your shoes. Another example is driving a car. Very little is going on consciously regarding driving. Think about having to consciously work the steering wheel: a little to the left, a little more, no, back to the right, now back to the left, . . . , argh it would drive you nuts! Your subconscious mind seems to be able to deal with a great many things at a much higher speed and much less effort than you can consciously.

Here is a table comparing some of the capabilities of our two "minds" capabilities (*next page*).

***Archery Implications*** Since repetitive tasks are in the province of the subconscious mind, we must train our subconscious "us" to do our shooting. The ancient Greeks had a saying that "Repetition is the

| Your Conscious Mind . . . | Your Subconscious Mind . . . |
|---|---|
| Can do only one thing at a time. | Can do hundreds of things at a time. |
| Tends to be your final decision maker (or seem to be). | Influences your decisions. |
| Has final say in matters of right and wrong. | Whatever . . . will guess for you. |
| Tells the subconscious what to learn. | Learns exactly what it is taught, but not what you think that is. |
| Acts on information brought up by the subconscious. | Filters out unnecessary information / highlights interesting information. |
| Is heavily focused on itself. | Can't distinguish between what is real and what is vividly imagined |
| Is relatively slow. | Is blazing fast. |

mother of learning" (All of my students just say it *is* a "mother.") and this certainly applies to archery, but look at this more carefully. If you were to go to the range every day and put on your headphones and shoot for two hours, would this make you a better archer? Most folks would say "yes," but it is actually "no." You would be a stronger archer as you would develop your archery muscles, but a better archer? Uh, unh, nope. (Bubba, at least take off your ear buds while you are reading this, sheesh!)

To train your subconscious mind to make good shots and only good shots, you must *focus* on what distinguishes a good shot from a bad one. You must let down any shot that deviates from your shot sequence (the Rule of Discipline!) and you must correct any mistakes that occur. The very worst thing that can happen to you is to make a mistake and then have the arrow go into target center. I am sure you have felt that relief when you made an obviously poor shot that scored well. Fine. Now what? You have just told your subconscious mind that it is okay to improvise as long as the outcome is good! This is bad juju . . . very bad.

You need to watch out because your subconscious mind has its own agenda. One of its jobs is keeping you alive by conserving your energy for you. If any task can be done using less energy, then less food

71

is needed to keep you alive . . . a good thing. Consequently, if you flub up a shot and it required less energy than your normal shot, it is a double whammy; your subconscious mind will be hot to repeat this new, *better* (meaning "requires less energy") shot.

In just the last few years it has been learned that your subconscious mind apparently approaches any task as if it were, at least in some small part, new. (This is for the same reason that you can't focus on just one thing for more than a few seconds; if the subconscious could be perfectly programmed to execute the exact same task over and over, predators would learn to trigger the behavior and then, knowing exactly what the response would be, dine on their prey—you!) So, you must *reinforce* what is a good shot over and over because it never, ever becomes fully automatic.

One more time . . . you must reinforce what is a good shot over and over because it never, ever becomes fully automatic. I could say it again, but I think you get it. This is really important!

Reinforcing what is a good shot is done emotionally. That's right, you need to use your emotions, so dust them off and make sure their tanks are full of gas.

When you shoot a shot well, *you must feel good about it.* When you shoot a shot poorly, *you must disapprove.* But, you do not want these emotions to be strong! Jumping around and chest bumping people on every good shot will soon wear you out (and probably get your rear end kicked in by the other archers). You want the approval and disapproval to be mild. (My emotional role models are: for approval—Mr. Spock ("Fascinating.") and for disapproval—a spinster piano teacher ("That was not good, child, do it over."))

Feeling *strong* emotion on a bad shot brings even more attention of your subconscious onto that event. (Of course, I know you have never done that, I mean going ballistic because you shot a bad shot; that is so childish! Mature adults just don't do such things, do we?) When you go off because you shot a crummy shot, you have just turned that crummy shot into a "big deal." It is now so important your brain moves it from short term memory where it would have just faded away into medium/long term memory where it will be remembered. Great! Now you have a memorized template for shooting a bad shot! Don't do this!

Invoking strong emotions and associating them with a shot is a form of imprinting that actually makes that mistake easier to repeat!

You need a *calm* focus on what is and what is not "good" on each and every shot. This takes the form of *calm* approval or *calm* disapproval and each shot must be so reinforced.

So, wearing headphones and listening to music while you are shooting? Not a good idea as that can only distract you and/or, worse, cause emotional responses that have nothing to do with the shots you are making. You can be making bad shot after bad shot while the music is making you feel good. (Danger, Will Robinson! Danger!) Listening to music you hate can be a good drill to learn how to focus in the presence of distractions, but only a little of this needs to be done.

Shooting when you are distracted is bad. (Bad, Bubba, bad!)

Shooting when you are tired is bad, except on a few occasions where doing this can help you learn how to fight through fatigue. (Interestingly enough, if you are tired or out of focus, you can shake these off mentally. Try it!)

Because you train your subconscious abilities consciously, and you can concentrate on only one thing at a time, *archery practice must focus on only one thing at a time.* If you are changing equipment or form or execution . . . you must work on one thing at a time . . . one thing only. (If you don't give in and accept this, I'm gonna repeat it again!) Another key to this is when you are drilling, you need to *evaluate each drill only on what is being drilled!* If you are working on your bow hand and you accidently punched off a shot into the ceiling but with a really good bow hand, that is consider a good rep! You can't train your bow hand by giving it feedback on your release hand! Besides, focusing a little too much on one part of your shot will allow other parts to drift off, so you aren't expected to do everything else perfectly while drilling! This is also why most drills are done blank bale. Targets give feedback archers can't ignore. (But target good! Yes, Bubba, I know.) And the feedback the target is giving doesn't have anything to do with the drill you are doing. Take it down while doing drills.

Practice must be sharp and focused on what you are doing and only on what you are doing. Your shot sequence provides a framework for your mental program and you must be focused on executing that continually.

The benefit long term is that once you have built your shot and drilled it home, you will need far less practice to stay sharp than you needed to build your shot in the first place.

## Okay, Now . . .

Okay, here's how to create a killer mental program. And just to let you know right now—I cannot *give* you a mental program, *nobody can*. What works for one guy or gal won't necessarily work for you. You have to try a lot of things to find what works for you and then you have to practice them. Really, if somebody says "Here is what to do mentally . . ." and you do it, it might work. But will it work *best* for *you*? You won't know unless you test these things out.

Sound familiar?

Sound like it's just like dealing with archery equipment?

Sound like it's just like dealing with archery technique?

It is.

*The Pieces* The most common mental tools needed by archers are: awareness, positive self-talk, goals (process and outcome), affirmations, and visualization/imagery. Here are short descriptions:

*Awareness* Consider any bad habit you have had: at first you didn't know you were doing it, but then after it was pointed out you noticed when you had done it, then you noticed it just after you had done it, then you noticed it as you were doing it, then you noticed it just before you were about to do it—that was when you could correct that habit and not until then. This true for everyone. Becoming aware of a problem involves being aware of it in space and also in time.

Becoming aware of your body in space is really, really important because you can't see yourself shoot. (No, Bubba, not *outer* space, I am talking about just being aware of your body in the space around it.) You want to be able to "play back" a shot to feel and see every part of it immediately after shooting (the memories of the feelings fade in about 30 seconds, so be quick about it). If you can't do this, you need to practice doing it.

If you are unaware of what you are doing while shooting, you don't stand a chance against the guys who are. So, during practice, see if you can replay each shot in your mind immediately after shooting. If you can't; keep trying until you can. (You can do it, Bubba, si se puede!)

*Positive Self-Talk* Positive Self-Talk is simply being positive in all comments you direct at yourself. "I am such an idiot" is an example of *negative* self-talk. "I can do this!" is an example of positive self-talk. As the old saying goes: "If you think you can or you think you can't . . . you are right." (Henry Ford is associated with this quote and if that old bastard said it, maybe it has some merit.) You really need to police your

74

self-talk. Good practice is every time you catch yourself saying something negative about yourself (whether out loud or silently in your head!), you must rephrase that statement into something positive.

Normally self-talk comes in when you are shooting fine and everything is going swimmingly and then some negative thought pops into your head, a thought such as when looking through your binoculars, you see a shot just low enough to be out of the top scoring ring and "Whoa, here we go again!" pops into your head. Maybe the shot is "in" or maybe it is "out" but one shot does not indicate a trend. A positive piece of self-talk to replace the above might be "I didn't expect to be perfect in this round and it is always a good sign when my misses are by tiny amounts. And I may have caught it outside-in, anyway."

Quick, Bubba, if a negative thought comes into your head, what do you do?

Uhh, let down?

You get an A, Bubba! The Rule of Discipline requires you to let down if there is any intrusion on your thinking from outside the shot and negative thinking is definitely one of those. (I am so proud of you!)

Negative thoughts are pounded into our heads from the minute we are born and can't be expected to just stop when we are shooting. When negative thoughts happen to you, you need to take a mental break and then rewrite that negative thought as a positive thought and think it to yourself with some feeling. Practice this, let's see, yeah, when you are awake. (I mean all the time, Bubba, all the time.) If you only practice this when you are shooting, your wallowing in negative thinking the rest of the time will make that practice almost useless.

*Goals (Process and Outcome)* Goals are obviously something you strive for. The distinction here is that outcome goals are ends in themselves: archers use these to create ladders to success (I want to win that small tournament, then a bigger one, then become state champion, then national champion, . . .). Process goals are goals describing the means to an end, that is to achieve an outcome. For example, "I will have a strong bow arm on every shot of this practice round" is a process goal.

Process goals are how you train yourself. To make a process goal work for you, take a page in your notebook and write the goal at the top of the page. Make a list of numbers down the page, one for each end. After each end, write down (you can just use tic marks) how many of the shots in that end included your goal behavior (like having a

75

strong bow arm). Then, before you go back to the shooting line, re-read the process goal at the top of the page. In this way, the process goal is reinforced each and every end so it doesn't get forgotten in the heat of competition, uh, practice (either actually). I can't say this strongly enough, if you have a process goal, you must evaluate each shot and make a written record (like hash marks, e.g. ⦀ ) of "how you did" at the end of each end of shooting. It is not enough just to *have* a goal, it must be evaluated and reinforced continually to provide the focus the goal needs to succeed. This is how to train yourself!

*Affirmations* Affirmations are statements in which you state a certain belief. Repeating these can help generate those beliefs. An example of an affirmation is: "I enjoy the pressure of competition; it means I am close to winning!"

*Visualization/Imagery* Visualization/Imagery is using one's imagination to help one shoot. This is most often employed during one's shot sequence by imagining a perfect shot just before shooting, and when something rattles you during competition, you can imagine you are shooting at home or in some other comfortable place to calm yourself. Most people use visualizations or imagery to implant in their minds what a good shot looks like and feels like (and sounds like, etc.; the more senses involved in the imagining, the better) before they shoot every shot on the belief that it is easier to repeat a complex task than do it from scratch. This is based on the idea that the subconscious mind cannot distinguish between what is real and what is vividly imagined.

If you are dying to know the difference between visualization and imagery, I will explain. (If not, skip to the next paragraph.) Psychologists state the difference is that visualizations only involve the sense of sight (the "visual," get it?). Imagery involves all of the senses in you imagining: sight, sound, smells, the whole kit and caboodle. Psychologists obviously have too much spare time on their hands. But, really, the more senses involved in a mental exercise, the more easily remembered it is, so maybe they have a point. I favor the "imagery" form. (Smell the greasepaint, clown, smell it!)

*Your Shot Sequence* I also include in this basic category your shot sequence because it provides a framework not only for the physical shot but for your mental program (while shooting) also. A shot sequence is the series of steps you undertake to execute a shot. This can be as simple as "#1 Draw, #2 Release" up to having well over two dozen steps. See Chapter 10. It provides a step-by-step route for your conscious attention during a shot. (But don't count off steps during shots, that is way too distracting. Shot sequences are for practice and troubleshooting, not a checklist for shooting an arrow.)

## The Process

Here is how you can create your own killer mental program. (Finally, jeez this guy goes on and on! Hey, who are you and what are you doing in my book?!)

*It Requires a Notebook* Duh, c'mon now, there is just too much stuff to remember! Yes, some guys do it without writing anything down. But why do it the hard way just because some guy who last read a book in the third grade did it that way? Adults take notes when they need to. (They don't have to be fancy. Your handwriting doesn't have to be good. Nobody is going to see your notes unless you show them, so loosen up a little and try this.)

*Getting Oriented . . . Mentally* First, you need to address some questions to help you "see the signs." Here they are:

1. *What stresses you mentally* (of course while shooting, not your girl friend or your mother-in-law, sheesh)? Make a list.

2. *How do you respond to those stresses?* Do you shake when you shoot? Do you palms get sweaty? Does your heart rate go up? Do you stop breathing during shots? . . . or pant like a dog? Do you get butterflies in your stomach? If you don't know these "signs" that you are getting stressed, you can slide into such situations and make mistakes before you can take action (first you don't know you are doing it, then . . . etc.).

3. *What is your normal level of arousal?* No, Bubba, we are not talking about sex here, we are talking about how calm you are while shooting. Archery is a "low arousal sport" (compare with being an NFL linebacker), but all sports have what is called an "arousal curve." Here's a generic one (*right*).

   If you are too hyped up, you won't perform

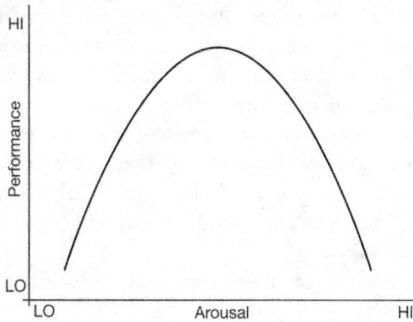

77

well. Similarly if you are too mellowed out, you won't perform well. And everybody's different! You need to know what your own normal arousal level, your normal level of intensity, is so that if you are too high or too low, you can adjust it.

And you can't tell this by just guessing, you have to note what you think it is over many shooting sessions to get a good read on how you are. You've spent a lot of years ignoring this, so it isn't going to just jump out and say "you are a 3.2 on a 0-5 scale!" Start thinking about it and take notes. Over time you will learn what works for you.

4. *How do you feel pressure?* All pressure symptoms come from you. What are they? How do you know you are "feeling pressure?" If you don't know what your "symptoms" are, how do you know how to cope with them? This isn't a one time thing, it is a little like taking someone's temperature when they are sick, you don't always get the same result. You have to take it over and over. And you have to take notes (like the nurses in the hospital always writing stuff on those clipboards). This is something that doesn't come up in practice, so you have to take notes *after* a tournament (during may be too distracting to your shooting).

5. *What things distract you during competition?* Do you really dislike poor lighting indoors? How about having to look into the face of a left-handed archer while shooting? Having your shooting partner suffering from gastric distress? (Whew!) What things get you out of your game? Break your concentration? Make a list and rank them from worst to least. Again, if you are aware of these things, you can deal with them. If not, you will find that you will have lost some number of points before you identify what is causing you to lose focus, and that is too late!

6. *What makes you confident?* I mean really confident. When you feel that your arrows are going right where they are aimed . . . when you feel like you can't miss. What causes that? Is it a feeling? Is it a string of good shots in a row? What is it?

I am not asking you to guess. I am asking you to become aware when in practice or competition you feel really confident. When you notice that you are feeling particularly confident take note of that, make a note or two and see over time whether the cause or causes are the same.

The key point here is: if you can figure out what encourages confidence in you, what would you do with that knowledge?

*Now Put Together a Mental Tool Set* This is just your first guess at what mental tools you want as part of your mental program. As a hint, most successful archers police their self-talk and use visualizations of perfect shots in their shot routines. The order I introduce mental skills to new archers is: first self-talk policing (Make it positive, Grasshopper!), next process goals, and third visualizing perfect shots (typically just before they raise their bow because there won't be time to do it after that and their "image" will fade quickly so it isn't something they can do earlier). Process goals aren't always involved when shooting, which is why most accomplished archers just mention self-talk (being positive) and visualization/imagery.

Whatever your tool set is, you must then take notes about how well these things work. Which means you have to practice them. And keep your ears open when people talk about the mental game. There are lots of tools not mentioned here and you might find one that sounds like it might work for you.

Here's how you go about figuring out whether they work, or not.

## Mental Practice

I imagine you are thinking: "When should I practice the mental part?" The answer is that the mental and physical are inseparable. The only mental tools that get separate practice are the "tools you use when things go wrong." Obviously you can't wait for things to go wrong (even though they seem to often enough) for opportunities to practice. At a bare minimum, I will go though my "disaster tool kit" whenever I am preparing for a tournament. *Note* Coaches or shooting partners can help out by creating "problems" for you in the middle of practice rounds and requiring you to adjust. ("Your bowstring (or D-Loop, or . . .) just broke. You have fifteen minutes to repair the problem and get sighted back in.")

The point here is that if you want to try visualization/imagery in your shot sequence, put it in your shot sequence and then do it *every arrow you shoot.* Same with policing your self-talk. There is no "I am going to do 15 minutes of mental practice every other practice session." Just start doing it: no exceptions, no time off, no shilly-shallying. Just do it.

And take notes. (I know, Bubba, life is hard, but if being really good at archery were easy, heck, everybody would be doing it.)

One good way to evaluate your "mental practice" is to create a form to fill out at the end of every practice/tournament. The form only needs a few questions to answer, for example "What percent of your shots included a visualization of a perfect shot before raising your bow?" (*Typical Answer* 85%, 90% . . . the goal being 100%, of course.) "Did you shoot better than average, worse?" (*Typical Answer* Felt really good, score was up 4-5 points over normal.) "How did you feel while shooting?" (Typical Answer: Shooting after work I was a little tired and being ticked off at my boss made it hard to focus . . . at first.)

Creating new habits takes time. The most oft quoted stat is that "it takes 21 days to create a new habit" (This came from the book "Psycho-Cybernetics" written by Maxwell Maltz in 1960. I haven't found any science to back this up, but hey, if you want to sound cool in archery, it makes a great quote.) *It takes effort and time to make a new habit and if you evaluate too quickly, you will get false results.* So, accumulate a couple dozen of these "debriefing forms" and then decide whether that mental skill improved your game or not.

Sometimes mental practice doesn't seem like it. Here's an example: at a recent indoor club shoot, the best shooter in this area ended up arriving without his quiver or his release aids. He had changed cars at the last minute and hadn't gotten everything transferred. After we tormented him with the usual teasing, he proceeded to borrow a floor quiver and one of the several release aids offered (he checked several during practice to find one to use during the competition). He shot the whole round with one of the borrowed releases and while his X-count suffered a little, he shot his normal perfect score. This is a fine example of mental practice. Instead of going home or just watching, this archer used the opportunity to practice his disaster routines. Using unfamiliar equipment can be disconcerting, but it is easier the second time than the first and the third is easier than the second. There are reasons this guy is the top archer in the region and him building up his mental toughness is one of those.

## Finishing Up

There are just a couple more things I need to add so I can feel like I didn't leave anything important out. (Bubba, if your lips are tired from all of this reading, take a nap and come back later.)

*Getting There vs. Being There* The last couple of your practice scores were right there, high enough to win the tournament you are focusing on. Are you ready? Maybe yes, maybe no.

Your performance is largely controlled by your *self image*. Your self image is a subconscious part of you that can be likened to who you think you are. Not the "who do you think you are?" scolding of your mother, but who you really think you are. Your self image is intimately linked to your chances of winning. (If you think you are a loser, you are. If you think you are a winner, well, maybe.) To explain this, consider two archers showing up at a major tournament: one is relaxed, confident, and is telling everyone he is shooting really, really well because he is; the other is tense, worried, and is telling everyone about his struggles. Which of these two guys has the better chance of winning? Duh. The confident guy. But, if the guy was faking all the confident behavior and talk: he isn't shooting all that well, the confidence and relaxed postures are all an act, then all bets are off. (And I sure wouldn't bet on that guy, either.)

The real winners appear confident and relaxed because they are confident and relaxed. They have a high expectation of winning because winning is something they do; they are winners. Their internal picture of themselves, their self-image, is that of a winner. These guys have a real edge.

So, how are you supposed to get your self image to look like theirs, without a lot of experience winning? Well, for one, you can't get there by lying to yourself or anyone else. You must first *convince yourself* that you can be expected to shoot winning scores any time you want. So, how many of those potentially winning practice scores do you need to create this winning self-image? Well, let me tell you a story about that. When I lived in California, my archery club had a weekly indoor league shoot at an archery shop every winter. I was still learning how to shoot compound unlimited/freestyle and one of these leagues used the NFAA five-spot target to shoot a 300 round. I started out this session shooting 296, 297, 296, 297, 298, and 298. So, the next six-week league I stuck to the same target, because I was really feeling I was "getting it" and I wanted to shoot a 300. So the next league started 298, 299, 298, 299, and 300! Cool! I even had 42 X's which was a new personal best X-count for me. Now, can you guess what my next score was? It was a 286. Talk about a smack down. I thought I had it made. A fellow club member hadn't shot anything but 300 on that round for over ten years. His self image was one that was telling him that he was a "300 shooter." My self image at that point was of a guy who got lucky and shot one 300 in his entire life. And I made the mistake of thinking doing it once meant I could do it any time.

81

Here's the thing. We all have *comfort zones* with regard to our performances. If we are performing way below what our self image is, we tend to get a little upset with ourselves and bear down and we perform better. I am sure you have experienced this. On the flip side, if we are shooting "lights out," way over our heads, something almost always happens to bring us down . . . down *and back into our comfort zone*, the one that includes shooting scores like that. It is close to being a form of personal sabotage. If you haven't experienced this before, just check out the performance of any pro golfer who has never won a tournament and is leading on the last day of a tournament. On very, very rare occasions, these newbies win. Much more often, though, they drop down the rankings like a stone. It is even worse when their playing partner on the final round is Tiger Woods (the Tiger Woods of 2009 and earlier). You couldn't count on him making more mistakes than you. And, gee, performing in front of these huge crowds is so different. And they are all cheering for him. Do you think those hopeful golfers include "Tiger Hunter" as some part of their self images? I would guess not.

When I learned about comfort zones, I thought back to the string of scores I described above. Before shooting the perfect score, I could remember making my first miss in several of those rounds and *having felt relieved!* The tension of trying not to miss had ended; I *was* relieved. This *was* more like me! But, argh! I didn't want *that* to be "just like me."

So, how do you change your self image to include you being capable of shooting winning scores? This is actually not that hard. Here is a technique I have heard from both Coach Bernie Pellerite and Lanny and Troy Bassham of Mental Management Systems. Let's say the goal is to become a consistent shooter of 300 scores on the NFAA 300 Indoor Round. You start with a five spot target set up at just five yards distance. (For you Bubba, that's five big steps.) Set your sight appropriately and shoot five arrows, aiming for the center of the X-ring but keeping your focus on shooting with good form and execution. Shoot the next five arrows. Now, if you miss the X-ring (or the spot, you can choose the level of the exercise), you must start over, from the beginning on a new target face. When you have shot 60 perfect X's (or spots), at your next practice you must do it again. After you have shot 3-5 perfect rounds this way, you can move the target out a couple of yards and repeat the drill. After you have shot 3-5 consecutive perfect rounds at that distance, you can move the target out to 10 yards and repeat the drill. Keep shooting and moving the target back until you are at regulation distance.

There are several different ways you can make this drill easier or harder. You can start with overlarge targets. You can use different distances. The key elements to keep in any variation is the building upon success and the "do over" requirements. If you can't get the perfect score or high score you are looking for, you made it too tough. Always start at a target size and distance you can shoot that perfect score (however you define "perfect"). When you have gotten back to the formal competition distance and formal target size and have shot 3-5 perfect scores, you will also have shot dozens of perfect scores. You will be quite used to shooting perfect scores. You will be quite used to shooting arrows into the X-ring.

The point is to shoot perfectly you must start at a distance at which this is easy and prove to yourself you can do it, become comfortable with doing it consistently. Then stretch out the difficulty just a bit and do it some more. This does work; I recommend it to you. Use caution, though, if you can't shoot 300 or close to 300 already, this is asking too much from a simple process. Also, you are going to learn a lot about focus and concentration. The first time I did this drill, I felt it was so easy that I got bored and missed . . . on the second end!

So, will your self image change through such a regimen? The answer is yes. Can it still be improved? The answer is yes. You have yet to prove to yourself that you consistently shoot 300 under tournament conditions, while traveling and eating fast food, etc. But to become a consistent winner, you have to win . . . and to win you have to *believe* you can win. Proving you can shoot arrow after arrow in the center of your target *to yourself* is the first part of this journey.

**Mental Traps** I can't end this section without warning you about some mental traps that archers can fall into. They are based in the psychological phenomena called cognitive dissonance and confirmation bias. (I just lost Bubba; I knew it. Dang.)

*Cognitive Dissonance* As with all things psychological, there is no "proof" of the existence of anything, but the concept of cognitive dissonance seems to ring true. Cognitive dissonance is just that whenever we hold two incompatible beliefs at the same time, we will distort one or the other or both so that they can live together. The classic example in archery is when you attend a competition thinking you have a good chance to win even though your scores aren't really good enough. The dissonance is set up around the typical winning score, let's say a score of 540 in an NFAA Field Round, and the fact that your average score is around 510. The odds of you shooting 35 points over your average are, like, zero. This is proven by the fact that you shot only one score over 530 in the last ten years. So, the vast majority of your scores are sub 540, but you will fixate on that 539 you shot, thinking "It could win for me!" You pay no attention to the "the 506 score I shot last week will lose for me" thoughts. You can delude yourself to the degree that when you lose, you will feel disappointed. In reality, you had no chance of winning.

Whenever two thoughts clash with one another (basically both can't be true; they are incompatible) everyone tends to bridge the gap between those thoughts until they can live together.

*Confirmation Bias* Confirmation bias was described in a song by Paul Simon ("The Boxer") in which he wrote "still the man hears what he wants to hear and disregards the rest...." We're that man! (Okay, or woman.) Once we have bought a new release or made any other major purchase, we don't want to feel that we have made a bad decision, so when we hear something good about what we bought, that sticks in our mind. If something bad about our new release is said, it slides through our minds like a hot knife through butter or we contest the information (That can't be true; you didn't hear that right!). This is normal human behavior and it applies to archery in small and large ways. For example, a dear friend was told she had a good finger release. She liked hearing this and even repeated it herself. Consequently no work was done to make her release any better or even different. Comments to the contrary were not heard. Finally, high-speed video showed that her release was a dead release followed by a beautiful, although fake, followthrough of the release hand.

More commonly, people invest a great deal of money in bows or arrows or whatever and then only hear things that confirm their good judgment and certainly nothing about the object's shortcomings. Obviously you can't compensate for shortcomings if you don't know what they are.

You need to be aware of these *general* human tendencies and they do apply to your archery. A major reason that you need to make written records and do actual tests to see if changes in your form, execution, or equipment really made improvements, is it is very easy to fall prey to what psychologists call the *Hawthorne Effect*. Basically, the Hawthorne Effect is that *anything done with the goal of making things bet-*

*ter will actually make things better . . . for a short time.* This was discovered over 50 years ago in a study of office work conditions. In that study office workers were told that a change was being made in office lighting that should make their work easier. Lo and behold, after the lighting was brightened just a bit, productivity increased. Then they were told that another adjustment should make things even better and the lights were dimmed back to their original level. Dumbfounded the researchers observed another productivity increase! This almost sounds too good to be true but reality reasserts itself in that the effects are gone after just a few days and things go back to normal.

Here's how the Hawthorne Effect applies to you. How many times have you gotten a new archery gizmo and decided within a day or even an hour or so that those new arrows, that new bow, etc. made a real improvement in your shooting. Well, they/it may have done that but it may also have lasted only a day or so. So, *after you have gotten used to your new thingamabob,* you need to do a group test or standard round test to see if there is any real improvement or whether you are just deluding yourself.

Written records are your ally in this! If you think you have made just so much progress but you look back a year or two and find out that your scores haven't really changed, you have a way to really tell what is going on. Your memory is always susceptible to cognitive dissonance and confirmation bias and it cannot be trusted.

*Mind Games and Trash Talking* There are competitors who will try to throw you off your game by playing mind games: disrupting your thinking, your pre-competition routine, arguing with you over a shooting lane on the practice field, etc. As much as possible you do not want to engage these people in any of their shenanigans. (No, Bubba, you cannot just beat them up. We represent a nonviolent archery organization.) The reason you need to avoid or not respond to these people is there is no upside, nothing to gain from it. I once asked Rick McKinney whether he or Darrel Pace, who were winning everything in Olympic-style archery in the 70's and 80's, ever engaged in mind games. His response was "no" in that he wanted his competitors to know they couldn't beat him, even on their best days. Wow, talk about arrogance . . . I like it!

It is somewhat traditional during friendly competitions to engage in a little "trash talking." For example, at one of our club's shoots a member brought with him a medal for a friend that he had picked up for him. When presenting his friend with his second place medal he said, "If you want to see what the first place medal looks like, I can show you mine. Have you ever seen one?" Now, this was all good natured ribbing between friends, but it can become harder edged when the competition gets a little hotter. I recommend that you do not engage in trash talking . . . while you are shooting. Save up your really good material for meals or meetings, etc. It is much too easy to let such talk get under your skin, causing you to lose your focus while shooting.

## The Capstone of a Mental Program

One of the most important aspects of an archer's mental program is that which allows him or her to always shoot in rhythm. (Okay, Bubba, we're back to talking about time and timing your shots.) Some archers shoot quickly, some shoot slowly. Fast archers who try to shoot slowly or slow archers who try to shoot quickly will only find disappointment. I am convinced that whatever your rhythm is, it is what it is and trying to change it is a fool's errand. You need to shoot in your rhythm. The task is becoming consistent at *your* particular rhythm.

*Finding Your Rhythm* This is the hard part. You either need to have someone with a stopwatch help you or possibly you can use a metronome to figure it out. In the stopwatch approach, you have somebody time how many seconds (without you noticing them doing it) it takes from raising your bow to releasing the string (or any two well defined points, with your shot between them). After each shot, you say "yes" if the shot felt good and was in rhythm or "no" if it didn't feel good or was out of rhythm.

After recording the times and arrow scores of many dozens of shots from more than one session, you try to correlate the number of seconds to the quality of the shot. One way to do this is to enter the number of seconds, arrow scores, and the yes's and no's into a three-column spreadsheet, sort the rows for time and see if the yes's cluster around any particular shot time. Do the good arrow scores cluster around any particular shot time? Do the good scores correlate with the "yes" ratings? (You are basically asking the question: "Am I a good judge of whether I am in rhythm?") For the sake of this discussion, let's say that most of the yes's and good arrow scores were from 4-6 seconds. This, then, is an indicator of your shot rhythm and there are now a number of ways to lock in that rhythm (see below).

The metronome approach to finding your rhythm is to play a

metronome and count off your shot, so many "clicks" for each step of the shot sequence. (The numbers will vary because the steps are not the same length.) If the metronome is set too fast, you will feel rushed or unable to count fast enough. If it is set too slow, you will feel sluggish and impatient. Eventually you get it set right and then you have found the rhythm you want to lock in. This can be confirmed by arrow scores shot at various test rhythms: the best rhythm should produce the better scoring arrows.

*Locking in Your Rhythm* There are a couple of ways to lock in your personal shot rhythm. One way is through feedback. Again, you need somebody with a stop watch. If your slice of time is 4-6 seconds from raising to bow to loose, your helper practices with you and times each shot. If you shoot quicker than the four seconds, he tells you. If you reach 6 seconds before shooting, he announces "let down" and you *must* let down the string. The feedback eventually gets you to shoot in your best rhythm. You will need several sessions to do this and you may need to test yourself at intervals to check on your status.

Another method is to use a personal metronome (they clip on to your ear) and practice in your rhythm. You can't necessary use it in competitions, though, so check your organization's rules. (Bubba forgot to take his off one time and complained about a ticking noise for almost three days!)

Yet another method is you may have a snippet of music in your head that is in the same tempo as your shot rhythm (or you may hear it and recognize it then). A great many archers use a sample of a song as part of their shot sequence. It helps them to stay in rhythm.

The End
*Now Go Forth and Suck No Longer!*

Steve Ruis

# Appendix

## But Wait, There's Still More!—
## This is Just Part of the Whole Story

What we have been just talking about is the mental program used while shooting, but the mental side of archery is quite big and it isn't just what is going on in your head while you are shooting. A mental program is the sum of all of the tools you will use mentally for competition. I break these down into three sets:

1. tools you use while shooting normally
2. tools you use when things go wrong, and
3. tools you use when planning/preparing.

All of these are needed and the key thing is they are needed now. (Actually you needed these a while back, but you missed that bus when it came by.) No delay is acceptable. Too often archers discover mental programs only when they are in competition and they are getting beaten and in desperation they think there is some mental hoodoo that will save their bacon. Unfortunately, this is another manifestation of archers believing in magic. ("There you go again!" *Ronald Reagan*) There is no mental hoodoo. There are mental skills which, *once learned* and *if practiced*, can make it very much more likely you will have a good day rather than a bad day.

The mental tools used when shooting normally (as described above), will make a large difference in your shooting, to the point you will not suck at archery any more. But if you want to know a little more about the whole picture, well, this is what this appendix is for. (No, Bubba, an appendix is not just the cause for a medical operation, it just means something added on at the end.)

*Tools You Use While Shooting Normally* There are mental tools that you can use while shooting and competing normally. That's what the whole of Section 2 is about.

*Tools You Use When Things Go Wrong* Here is where you earn your wings. What happens when you shoot a shot and you expected a 10 and got a 6 (or an X and got a spot or a five and got a four, whatever)? That is, what happens when things go wrong? There are three possible sources of a bad shot:

a. you

b. your equipment, and/or

c. the external environment (wind, birds, etc.)

Well, which was it . . . the source of that 6? This is your problem.

*Rational Troubleshooting* When trying to figure out a bad shot, if you allow your emotions to take over, you lose. You have only so much time to figure out what went wrong and correct it for the next shot. Spending time getting upset and then calming yourself back down doesn't solve the problem.

The first thing I do is mentally is I replay the shot in my mind. Did I try to "help" the shot and push it over into the 6-ring? Did I drop my bow arm? What questions get asked depends on whether the shot was high, low, left, or right. If high, left, or right I certainly am not going to check to see if a dropped bow arm was responsible as that would account only for a low shot. To do this accurately, I need to have a short list of things to check for each direction of misses. Here's a sample (*see diagram opposite page*).

But winning archers don't have generic lists, their lists include the cause of such shots based only upon what *they* are likely to do. So, start taking more notes in that notebook you bought.

If my "instant replay" of my shot doesn't indicate a reason for the problem, I next check for environmentals. If there is a wind flag, which direction is it blowing? If no flag, check the trees and bushes for signs of the wind. Did the wind gust during the shot? Does that account for the problem? And so on.

If not, I then check over my equipment, looking for loose arrow rests, loose sight blocks, something that would cause the problem. I do this last because I have checked, double checked, then triple checked my equipment to make sure it wouldn't fail, plus I am sensitive to things being "different" about my equipment. 9See, Bubba, being sensitive is not so bad!)

If none of these come up with a cause of the problem, I have to put the problem out of my mind and shoot another shot. If I don't put the last shot out of mind, thinking about it will probably mess up my next shot and

**Arrows Hitting High**
• nocking point too low
• bow "heeled"
• draw elbow too high
• bow drawn too far
• jerking up on release
• sight set wrong

**Arrows Hitting Left**
• aiming with wrong eye
• arrows too stiff
• floating anchor
• arrow slid off rest
• string hit armguard
• sight set wrong

**Arrows Hitting Right**
• arrows too weak
• bow canted (w/sight)
• pushed bow right
• plucking string
• sight set wrong

**Arrows Hitting Low**
• bow arm dropped
• nocking point too high
• arrow fell off of rest
• string hit armguard
• arrow nocked above locator
• sight set wrong

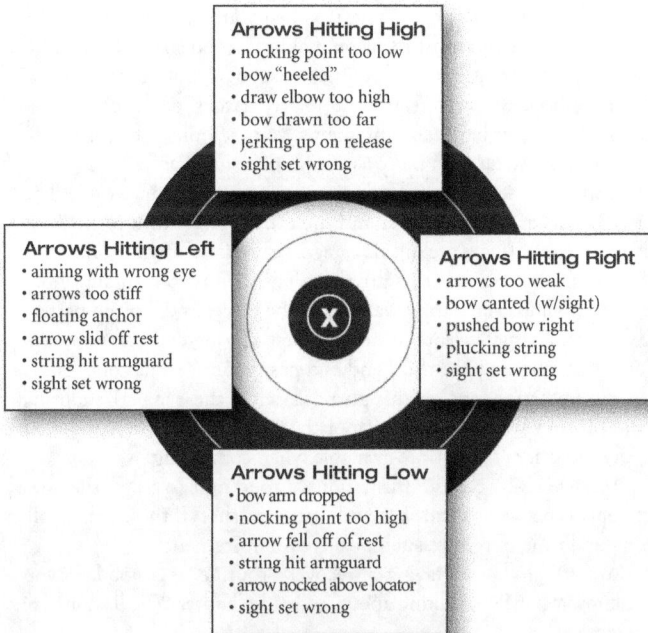

I will get neither a good score nor the information I need to continue.

You must learn to troubleshoot "bad shots" in such a way that you can minimize the damage. (This is a large part of "scoring well.") If you are lucky enough that a bad shot only costs you a few points and it is relatively early, you can catch up to a winning score. If it is late and very costly, you will probably be "out of luck." Sometimes, those are the breaks of the game.

*Visualizations/Imagery* What if the poor shot was due to one of the things you tend to do wrong? You have just executed incorrectly, now what? If you focus on what you did wrong, it just makes it more likely that you will repeat that incorrect execution.

To help you understand, think about what you do when you flub tying your shoelaces. Do you go back through the steps, walking through them methodically (*Step 1* Cross the laces, *Step 2* ...)? No, that's stupid, you merely focus a bit more on the task at hand, that is you avoid distracting thoughts or activities and then you simply tie your shoe.

91

This is what you must do in archery. When you have made a mistake, on your next shot you must focus on making a good shot . . . a little bit more. Very important in this is to imagine a good shot in your normal sequence especially vividly. You must not "try harder" or any other foolishness. When you have tense moments, your response needs to be to relax, not to tense up even more as a form of "trying harder."

A special case of this are folks who start tournaments weakly. The first 2-3 shots are shaky at best and then they settle down to shoot as they are capable. If you are in this category there is a visualization exercise you can use to avoid this problem. The drill is to mentally shoot the first two ends (including walking to the target and scoring perfect ends) in your visualization. When the first scoring end comes, it will be as if you were on your third end and past your nervous zone. Some people use practice ends for this purpose (when these apply), shooting them as if they were scoring. Both of these techniques can work . . . if you practice them so they are available when competing.

*Affirmations* If you use affirmations, a good time to repeat the ones that apply is between a bad shot and your next shot. If these help at all, it is a good time to receive such positive reinforcement.

*Recovery Strategies* Having a "recovery routine" is a good. If you don't know what I am talking about, go read Chapter 25. I'll wait here until you get back.

*Tools You Use When Planning/Preparing* I have already beaten you about the head and shoulders about not making any plans for practice, but the more seriously you want to take your archery, the more planning you have to do. Think about attending major tournaments, since these are often multi-day tournaments, you need to plan vacation days from work, you need to plan travel, lodging, food, and all kinds of other stuff. Several of your mental tools are useful in planning and preparing, and in fact, you would profit from considering planning to be a mental tool itself. Here are the two most useful mental tools used for planning.

I don't have the space to go over everything needed, like a calendar, and you can get someone else to do that stuff for you, so I am just going to address the planning aspects that affect your shooting.

*Outcome Goals* Let's say your goal for the season is to place in the top ten in the USAA outdoor nationals at the end of the summer. From the internet you consider that a FITA Round score of 1300 would be sufficient to guarantee that placing. If your current FITA

Round score is 1220, what should your goal be? If you answered 1300, you need a better grasp on what goals do for you! When was the last time you got a 80 point improvement in your average score on this round? (*Answer* Probably never.) When you set goals, they need to be clear and achievable. Maybe your first goal is to get your average score to 1240. Then maybe to 1260, 1280, and finally to 1300. These goals make a "ladder to success."

A goal of 1240 when you already shoot a 1220 sounds easy enough, but what are you going to do to make that change? If it were all that easy, wouldn't you have done it already? Ah, here is the rub. You now have to figure out what you will be doing differently to make a 20 point difference in your average score.

If you sit down with your coach and a pad and pen, you can probably come up with a list of things. Then you have to start trying them and see which of them actually make improvements. But the point here is, which feeling will you rather have:

a. I only have another 20 points to make my goal of 1300, but I met the 1240 goal, and the 1260 goal, and the 1280 goal; I can make this one, too!

*or*

b. I only have another 20 points to make my goal of 1300, but I have had this goal all summer and I am running out of time; I am not going to make it.

Working your way up a ladder, one rung at a time, rather than trying to make one giant leap, provides you with a series of successes that enables you to gauge your progress as well as convince you that you can meet goals. Hey, that's why they build ladders they way they do.

*Affirmations* Affirmations can be written on 3x5 cards and stashed around your house or apartment (on your dresser, on the mirror in your bathroom, on the fridge, etc.). Every time you encounter a card, you stop and read it (out loud is best). This guarantees that these positive thoughts about the "you" you want to become are reinforced several times a day. (If you want an inspiring story involving affirmations, look up Billy Mills' story of how he got his Olympic Gold Medal in the 10,000 meter race.)

Planning tools are almost entirely mental and are a great help in getting you onto the winner's platform.

## **Postscript**

If you want to learn more about mental skills for archery I am working on another book tentatively titled "The Archery Focus Big Book of Mental Skills." Look for it if you are interested. If you can't wait, the best thing to read right now is Lanny Bassham's "With Winning In Mind."

*Steve Ruis*
Chicago, IL
Fall 2012

## Notes

_____

_____

_____

_____

_____

_____

_____

_____

_____

_____

_____

_____

_____

_____

## Notes

_____

_____

_____

_____

_____

_____

_____

_____

_____

_____

_____

_____

_____

_____

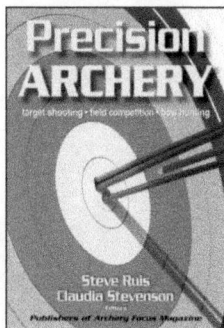

Steve Ruis

www.ingramcontent.com/pod-product-compliance
Lightning Source LLC
LaVergne TN
LVHW021537080426
835509LV00019B/2692